HOW TO SAVE MONEY WITHOUT REALLY TRYING

A Step-by-Step Guide To Saving $1,000 Per Month

KATE ROBINSON

Copyright © 2016

All rights reserved. No part of this publication should be produced, stored in a retrieval system or transmitted in any form or by any means: electronic, mechanical, recording, or otherwise without the prior written permission of the authors.

Disclaimer
This e-book has been written for information purposes only. Every effort has been taken towards making this e-book as true, complete and accurate as possible. However, there may be mistakes in typography or content. Also, this e-book provides information relevant to carefully selected online money spinning business ideas only up to the publishing date. Therefore, this eBook should be used as a guide – knowing that new information is constantly coming up.

The purpose of this eBook is to educate. The author and the publisher do not warrant that the information contained in this e-book is fully complete and shall not be responsible for any errors or omissions. The author and publisher shall have neither liability nor responsibility to any person or entity with respect to any loss or damage caused or alleged to be caused directly or indirectly by this e-book.

First Edition: September, 2016.

CONTENTS

Introduction	9
How To Manage Your Money to save $1000 per Month	10
Saving Money Automatically with Digit	12
How does it work?	12
Digit saves a little every week	12
Access your savings anytime	13
Budgeting	13
Your current situation	14
Keep a record of all expenses	15
Balancing the accounts	18
Paying Bills	19
Paying the utility companies	22
Standing Order	23
Direct Debit	23
Cutting Costs : Water Meters	23
Start saving $1,000 per Month	25
Create a Penalty Jar	25
Stop Loaning Money to Uncle Sam	26
Conquer The 5% Challenge	27
Set a Strategy For The Supermarket	27
Improvise For Income	28
Be Fanatical About Fees	29
Review Your Technology	29
Rethink Your Recurring Expenses	30
Forget About Brand Names	31
Be Smarter About Using Credit Cards	31
Optimize Your Cell Phone Bill	32
Create a 'No Spending' Day Once A Week	32
Sell One Thing On eBay	33
Only Buy Something New When You're Replacing Something Old	33
Use Psychological Barriers To Prevent Yourself From Spending Money	34

Pay Money To Save Money   35
Use The Free Rewards From Your Credit Card, Car Insurance, and Workplace   35
Earn More Money Using a Skill You Already Have   36
Use Coupons   36
Don't Ignore the Surveys   37

How to save A thousand dollars per month on Groceries   39

Save Money on Groceries at Home   39
   Use what you have before buying more   39
   Get the most out of the food you prepare   40
   Plan a menu   40

Get the Best Price   40
   Look for sales and coupons   40
   Get a store card   41
   Use a credit card that offers cash back rewards on groceries   41

Ways to Save Money While Shopping in Grocery Stores   42
   Check unit prices   42
   Buy generic   42
   Look toward the top and bottom of shelves   42
   Minimize purchases of convenience foods   43
   Avoid single serving items   43
   Buy in-season fruit and vegetables   43

Purchases Patters To Avoid   44
   Avoid impulse buys   44
   Eat before you shop   44
   Only buy groceries   44
   Don't buy small if you can buy in bulk   45

Ways you use Waste dollar rather than saving it   46

Extended Warranties   46

What you should do	47
Paying More Than You Have To On Gas	*47*
What you should do	48
The Cost of Brand-Name Items	*48*
What you should do	48
Uused Memberships	*49*
What you should do	49
That New Car Smell	*49*
What you should do	50
Credit-Monitoring Fees	*50*
What you should do	50
Unnecessary Insurance Coverage	*51*
What you should do	51
Items You Won't Use	*51*
What you should do	52
Impulse Buys	*52*
What you should do	52
Interest Charges	*52*
What you should do	53

Ways you Flushed Money Down the Toilet Today   54

You Ate Out For The Third Time This Week	*54*
You Drove At 80 mph To Get To Work	*55*
You Drank Half A Bottle Of Wine And It's Only Wednesday	*56*
You Chose Plastic Bottled Water	*56*
You Were Too Lazy To Cut Out A Coupon	*57*
You Let Your Belly Rumblings Prod You To The Vending Machine	*57*
You Spent Half An Hour Reading About Things You Already Know	*58*

Reasons you need to save up Money for Future   59

Emergency Funding	*59*
Retire In Peace	*60*
Fewer Debts	*60*
Financial Independence	*60*

Buying a House	61

Ways To $1,000 per month Save Money in college   62

Make a Budget, Check It Twice	62
Rule the School	63
Recycle	63
Shack Up	64
Cook It Up	64
Shop Around	65
Free Yourself	65
Rent, Rent, Rent	66
Reciprocate	66
Plan Ahead	67
Maximize Summer	68
Start Small	68
Stay Put	69
Carpool	69
Give Back	70
Trade In	70
Pay the Interest	71
Can It on Credit	72
Work Hard	72
Tap Hidden Money Resources	73
Ask for More	73
Access Student Discounts	74
Get Personal With the Career Center	74
Work it Off	75

Ways College Students can save $1,000 per month before Class Starts   76

Buy Textbooks Used	76
Ask About Student Discounts	77
Find Free or Cheap Transportation	78
Call Your Roommate to Avoid Duplicate Purchases	78
Choose the Meal Plan That Works for You	79
Research the Best Cell Phone Plan	79
Set up the Right Student Checking Account	80

Resource   **82**
  Create a Spending Plan   *82*
    Draw a Spending Map So You Don't Get Lost   82
  A Diet for Your Wallet!   *83*
    Part 1   83
    Step 1: Start with total monthly income: 83
    Step 2: Next, list your monthly expenses: 83
    Part 2   85

Conclusion   **88**

One Last Thing...   **90**

Introduction

This book is designed to help you in many ways. Its main objective is for you to save $1,000 per month. There are ways to save a little and other ways to make greater savings. Some require very little effort, others are not possible without a certain degree of sacrifice or compromise in your life, but this book focuses on effortless and effective ways to save money. Most of us do not earn as much as we think we need, and are constantly left wishing for that little bit extra. This eBook will not necessarily make you money, which is a different area altogether, but it will help you utilise what money you do have more efficiently. The eBook contains valuable advice such as how to make more efficient use of your energy and time, and useful tips such as the secrets of getting a bargain, plus general hints on other areas of life that can save you money.

Many readers have found the book to be key in helping them achieve their saving goals, and I hope it will be helpful to you as well.

How To Manage Your Money to save $1000 per Month

We have less and less real contact with our money these days. Salaries are normally paid directly into bank accounts because although there is nothing nicer than being handed a pile of cash it is more sensible and secure to have it paid in this way. This removes the temptation not to pay all of the money into the bank but to 'blow it all' straight away, and makes it easier to keep track of your finances.

The banks now offer services such as:
- Direct debit
- Standing orders
- Budget accounts

These enable many expenses such as gas or electricity bills to be paid directly from your account by the bank. Subscriptions to journals or clubs can also be debited directly, without the need for you to write regular cheques. The advantages of these types of services are that they save you time, and take out the worry of remembering to pay certain bills. This itself will save you money if you would otherwise be financially penalized for an overdue bill that had slipped your mind.

Paying with cash is becoming a thing of the past: even cheques are now being superseded by debit and credit cards in all but the smallest transactions. The general effect of 'paying with plastic' is to increase demand. Plastic does not feel like money, and the time delay between paying by credit card and actually receiving the bill means that many people spend more than they can really afford simply because it is so easy to do so. When the bill arrives, they are only asked to pay a minimum of, usually, 5% of the balance. This does not feel 'painful', and encourages full use of available credit.

Never borrow more than you can comfortably repay

Unfortunately, credit cards are an expensive way of borrowing. A prearranged overdraft at a bank is a cheaper way of borrowing than a balance on a credit card, and if your card balance becomes uncomfortably high you could save money in interest payments by paying off the card balance either with money from an overdraft or from a loan. If credit cards are used with restraint, however, they can save you money. If your bank account is not in credit and you wish to purchase something, buying it with a credit card gives you at least a month's interest free credit. If you then pay the balance in full at the end of this interest free period, it means you have avoided paying a little extra interest on your overdraft during this period.

Saving Money Automatically with Digit

While the internet is a dangerous way to spend more money with the access to thousands of online stores right from home, it can also be used to help you save money without any effort.

How does it work?
Every few days, Digit checks your spending habits and removes a few dollars from your checking account if you can afford it. To use Digit, you need to connect your checking account. This allows Digit to analyze your income and spending, and find small amounts of money it can safely set aside for you. They use 256-bit bank-level security, and they don't store your bank login.

Digit saves a little every week
Every 2 or 3 days, Digit transfers some money (usually $5-50) from your checking account to your Digit savings. They never transfer more than you can

afford, so you don't have to worry about over-drafting your account. In fact, they have a no-overdraft guarantee.

Sign Up to Digit: www.digit.co

Access your savings anytime
They know you're saving for good reasons – a trip, a big purchase, or even just a rainy day. When you need your savings, send Digit a text message. Digit will transfer the money from your Digit savings back to your checking account next business day. Digit allows unlimited transfers, with no minimums, and no fees.

Budgeting

In an ideal world it would be nice not to have to worry about money. However, it appears that regardless of how much we earn we spend right up to our limit and often over it. No matter how many possessions we own or how many holidays we take we always seem to want more. If you are not like this then you are lucky! We may not all be greedy, but it is human nature to want more. So the solution is to be more careful with our money. If you have an idea of exactly how you spend your income it will be easier to make adjustments to your expenditure. But as we seem to have little actual contact with our money it is often harder to control. That is the advantage of using cash as a primary method of payment: you can actually feel and see the money leaving you. This is always painful and you might be less inclined to fritter it away than if you were paying with a credit card.

The best advice if you cannot control your spending is to take a pair of scissors and cut up your cards and stick to paying with cash.

Your current situation

It is a good idea to begin your efforts towards saving money with a financial overhaul. The first stage is to work out what money you have coming in, if you have a partner do a joint calculation. Possible sources of income are, for example:

- Wages
- Pension
- Investment Income
- Income Support
- Sickness Benefit
- Invalidity Benefit
- Housing Benefit

The next stage is to try and work out what your expenses are for an average month. If you write down all your various expenses it is then easier to begin to think about cutting down in certain areas. If you have no record of what you have been spending it is much harder to do this. The best thing is to keep a written record of all expenses, covering everything during the next thirty days. Provided nothing too exceptional was bought during this period, it will be alright to use this as an average month.

Keep a record of all expenses

Many people are quite content to avoid all possible thought of how they spend their money because they feel guilty at what they have been spending their money on, or because they don't realise that by paying attention to where it goes they could save a fortune. If you write down and look carefully at your expenditure then you will be more inclined to make some sort of effort to make a few cutbacks. It is not always possible to account for every penny but here is a list of some of the most commonly incurred expenses:

- Food
- As well as the regular weekly shopping make a note of how much is spent on occasional snacks, drinks, sweets and meals out. This can often be equal to or in excess of the amount spent in the supermarket, and represents an area with huge potential for economizing.

- Motoring
- Travel expenses
- Household necessities: Mortgage or rent, council tax, phone bill, television licence, energy bills.
- Other necessities: Credit repayments, insurance, assurance etc.
- Entertainment
- Holidays
- Newspapers
- Saving
- Sundries

Also include a list of debts, such as money owed on:
- Credit cards
- Hire Purchase
- Overdrafts
- Loans
- Mortgages

Any money that is borrowed will be costing you money in interest. In some cases, extortionate rates of interest are charged. The above list covers a range of expenses. Some of them are referred to as fixed costs, such as mortgage repayments, council tax, hire purchase instalments, insurances etc. These fixed costs are normally paid at fixed times, so you know when to budget for the expense. The other type of costs is variable costs, and as their name implies they change according to usage, like heating or electricity. You should work out how much your fixed expenses are and set aside an appropriate amount of money for these, then you can work out how much you have to spend on the variable expenses, over which you have some control.

It is sensible to keep an accounts book, not just the back of an envelope, as being organized is one of the secrets of saving money.
Using past bills write down your expenses for the previous year, if available, in order to give you an idea of what to budget for the month. This is useful because some expenses are seasonally variable: gas bills, for example, are higher in winter than in summer, so knowing only what the average gas bill is may leave you short when the winter bill arrives as it will be way above average.

Past bills will give you an awareness of roughly what to budget for, taking into account inflation and other factors of course. Follow this guide for two years your lifestyle will ever be the same, but an approximate guide is better than no guide. The first step towards saving money when looking at the year as a whole is to have a reasonable idea of how much the main expenses will be. When budgeting for this year on the basis of last year, try to add a couple of percentage points above the rate of inflation in order to cover yourself against inevitable price rises.

Balancing the accounts

In theory the amount of money coming in should tally with the amount of money going out. However, this is living on the edge as there are always expenses which you cannot plan for and therefore savings are needed to cover these eventualities. For those who find surviving on their income a constant battle, remember you are not alone. In fact, getting into debt is not at all uncommon. If you are still in control of your debt, i.e. you can cover the repayments, then this is not so bad. But for many the debts spiral and can eventually lead to serious problems such as homes being repossessed or having the bailiffs enter your house and remove your possessions in order to recover bad debts. This is a devastating experience that should be avoided at all costs. In order to avoid slipping into the 'debt trap' keep a watchful eye on your expenditure and never borrow more than you can afford comfortably to repay. If you are struggling to save $1,000 per month, there are two simple choices:

- Choice 1 is to increase your income.
- Choice 2 is to reduce your expenditure.

Making the money you earn go further will have a similarly beneficial effect.

It all sounds easy in theory, but in reality whichever choice you make will require willpower and effort to achieve. Just remember that although changing your expenditure habits in order to avoid debt may not be easy, it is far easier to go out of your way to walk around a hole than to try to climb out of it once you have fallen in. Debt can be like that, and is better avoided in the first place. This eBook's aim is not really to tell you how to increase your income, but there are tips here and there throughout the book which may be of use.

Primarily it is concerned with choice number 2, reducing expenditure, but in a way that will not be painful, complicated or difficult. Anyone can make easy savings if they know how.

Paying Bills

A brown envelope popping through the letter box is rarely good news. In fact the majority of post seems to be either bills or junk mail, and the bills can cause a real headache if not downright despair. But if you are organised you will find that it is easier to make the payments, and paying on time will avoid penalties and save money. Most of the utility companies do not take it ease with late or nonpayment and their punishment for this sort of behavior is often to cut off the service they provide. This not only leaves you very inconvenienced but it will cost you even more money when you have to pay to be reconnected. Some bills, such as those for electricity and gas, are often worked out as an estimate. This means that the company calculates a new bill using past bills as a guideline to what amount they expect you to have used.

The first thing to do when you have opened your bill is to check the estimated figure with the true reading. If the estimate is way off the mark, either too high or too low then the money they are requesting will be wrong. Obviously if their estimate is much higher than the actual reading you will be paying more than you have to, and I'm sure you would rather have the use of that money yourself. If the estimate is only marginally out, there is no point in having your bill altered, but if it is a significant amount of money then you can send the company in question a true reading and they should send you a revised bill. If the bill they sent you is too low then you are not obliged to inform them, it just means that when they do read the meter your next bill will be that much larger, so be prepared. If the bill you receive is higher than you believe it should be, don't just accept it as being automatically correct as you could be paying more than you should. There was a case where a man received a phone bill for a period when he was away, he queried this with BT, and eventually they found that due to some faulty wiring his line and another person's had been mixed and for years they had been paying each other's bills.

There are thousands of queries every year for most of the utility companies, so it is certainly not a quick procedure getting something investigated. The company will often be adamant that there is no problem. Keep on persevering until they do listen, or contact the official body that governs their conduct if you have no luck. One common problem stems from inaccurate meters. If you believe the bill is higher than it should be it is usually possible to have the meter checked. However, there is a drawback to this approach: before you think about having this done, bear in mind that if the company checks the meter and they find there are no faults with it then you will have to pay them. This varies from company to company, but is around $20 to $30.

Paying the utility companies

Most people are connected to the electricity, water and gas supplies. Life would be exceedingly difficult without them, but these luxuries have to be paid for. Most of the companies send out quarterly bills, which have to be settled within a certain period. Some companies allow payment to be made through a direct debit scheme, which is convenient and can be cheaper if the company offers discounts for direct debit. There are also 'budget plan' schemes that are designed to spread the cost of your bills over the year, instead of having to pay them in large amounts. It sounds fine until you begin to think about it: instead of paying quarterly you will pay monthly instalments, and this means that you will be paying them in advance. It makes better financial sense to save the money yourself and put it in a savings account so that at least you get the interest on your own money before you pay the bill. The only advantage of these 'budget plans' is that they are helpful for people who find it hard to save or manage their finances.

Standing Order
This is an instruction that you give to your bank to pay a fixed amount from your account on agreed dates.

Direct Debit
This gives an organization the right to withdraw money from your account at agreed times. This is useful for paying for things such as car insurance.

Cutting Costs : Water Meters
It is now standard policy for many of the water companies to fit water meters so that they can calculate how much water a household uses and then charge according to usage. As with any change of policy it has aroused public concern. Prior to the water meters the bill was a fixed amount regardless of usage. There was no need to worry about using a sprinkler on the lawn and you could have as many baths as you had hot water. Sadly for many these days are over. For those who are cautious with their water supply, having a water meter might work out cheaper than the old system, but for many having to be economical with water usage is a burden. If you do not have a meter there is no compulsion to economize on water usage, however if you have a meter there will always be the thought that if you use less water the bill will be cheaper.

If you have a water meter and you want to cut your bill here are some tips:
- Take showers, not baths.
- Do not use a sprinkler on the garden.
- Use the washing machine only for full loads.
- Only use the dishwasher once a day.
- Mend dripping taps.
- Recycle water from the house and collect rain water in rain butts.
- Put a brick in the toilet cistern so that it uses less water to flush, or install a toilet with a dual flush system.
- Keep drinking water chilled in the fridge instead of running the tap until it is cold.

Start saving $1,000 per Month

Many Americans prefer to save money rather than spend it. Of course, saying and doing are two different things. Learn and adopt the smart ways to save $1,000 per month.

While the Great Recession was such a wake-up call that many do indeed save in a way they never had before 2008, people still lean on a pile of excuses for not saving as much as they would like or need to put away. But in reality, there are many ways to do it and do it well. I came up with areas you can cut back or be wiser with your money so that you can sock away $1,000 per month, based on our estimates.

Create a Penalty Jar

Maybe you have trouble giving up the goodies the little luxuries that add up. Give yourself a nudge by putting a penalty tax on your excess splurges. Take certain categories like your booze purchases, Starbucks pastries, manicures/pedicures, and cigarettes and match each receipt with a savings deposit.

For example, when you spend $20 for a mani-pedi, put that same amount into your secret stash until you build a tidy sum worthy of a trip to the bank. If you can't afford to save the matching amount that means you can't afford the treat. Assuming you're a big spender and adopt this method, you could become a big saver, as much as $200 or more a month.

Stop Loaning Money to Uncle Sam

"Your income tax refund is really an interest-free loan to IRS," says Jordan Niefeld, CPA at Gerstle, Rosen & Goldenberg, PA. In reality, it's your money you could have during the year to pay bills, reduce credit card balances and invest for your retirement. If your refund is $3,000, you could have about $250 more each month in take-home pay by adjusting your federal withholding.

If you get a sizeable refund at tax time, remember it's not a windfall, but instead a sign you need to review your W4. Determine whether you've selected the right number of withholding allowances. If you're getting a refund in the neighborhood of $2,000, figure that's about $167 a month you could instead put aside in your savings account to earn interest before tax time rolls around per year.

Conquer The 5% Challenge

There's no getting around taking a hard look at all your expenses, especially the discretionary ones. It's hard to go cold turkey and cut out entire categories of spending, but you can come up with a compromise. Can you stomach spending 5% less? If you're spending $400 a month, between lunches outside of the office, happy hour with co-workers, and restaurant and bar hopping with friends, you sure can. By spending just $20 less a month, over a year you'll save $240.

Set a Strategy For The Supermarket

One of the biggest budget busters can be the supermarket. Even a small family can easily rack up weekly grocery bills of $150-$200. If you can tame the supermarket lion, not only will you spend less time standing in line, you'll have a bit more in your pocket too. The only way to pull it off is with a plan. Always shop with a list and stick to it. Don't shop while hungry, or you'll buy all sorts of stuff you don't need. Take a hard look at coupons and fliers so you can get the best deals. And use a credit card that gives back money for your grocery shopping note that; some go as high as 6% that's a better return than what you'll get for a typical savings account.

Shop smarter and you can shave off at least $50 each week in out-of-pocket expenses.

Improvise For Income

"A side hustle is one of the best ways to increase your savings fast without sacrificing your lifestyle," says Sophia Bera, a Certified Financial Planner and founder of Gen Y Planning. Take advantage of opportunities that are right in front of you. Say you're a soccer mom or dad and you're always surrounded by other thirsty parents whose throats from dry from cheering. Next time, take a cooler full of bottled water that you got a great price on and sell it. Maybe you're handy at fixing things around your house. Don't be shy about letting people know, especially seniors and single mothers who may need assistance. Even a couple of service calls a month can mean more money for you to squirrel away. Consider too, whether there are opportunities for you to make money grocery shopping for neighbors and taking seniors to doctor's appointments, or taking other people's kids to their after-school activities. If you squeeze in just six free hours a week at $12 per hour, you can earn an extra $290 per month for your piggy bank.

Be Fanatical About Fees

If you look at all the fees in your life and find ways to eliminate them one by one well, you wouldn't feel like you hit the lottery, but you could have huge monthly savings. This includes the $2-3 you pay when you use an ATM other than your bank's and the late fees on credit cards that can be $20-$30 and more a month (and worse still if late payments cause your interest rate to rise). You may be paying a monthly fee for a checking account when other banks would be willing to give you one for free. Go through your financial accounts line by line, and you may be surprised by some of the fees you're paying. See what you can eliminate, consider switching service providers, and set up automatic payments if you are a chronic late payer. We bet you can be rewarded from this work with at least $75 per month.

Review Your Technology

In this much wired world, you have all manner of technology at your fingertips. Convenience isn't always cheap. Scrutinize your tech-related expenses. Are you getting the best deal on your cell phone package? Look around to see if there are new deals that make it worth switching. The same goes for your Internet service provider and cable television. How much television do you actually watch, and what channels are truly favorites? "Reassessing your cable or phone package could result in huge savings!" says Bera. "Ditch the cable for Hulu Plus and Netflix instead." At the very least, see where you can bundle services to get the best deal. It could also be time to get rid of your landline at home. A conservative estimate is a $100-per-month savings.

Rethink Your Recurring Expenses

Do a reality check. What do you have and what do you really use? If you're paying $75-100 or more a month for a gym membership and you haven't seen the inside of the gym in months, admit that you're no gym rat and put that money toward savings instead. Same goes for subscriptions. If you're not reading those magazines, cancel them. Review your car, life, and home or renter's insurance polices. Has anything in your life changed so that you should be paying less? Consider raising deductibles and ask about any "no claim discounts." Shop around for your insurance policies, and you may be able to save a few hundred dollars monthly. Assuming at least one of these areas is one you can trim, you could save $150 a month.

Forget About Brand Names

Being a label lover is a luxury. You can easily save 50-60% when buying generic at the grocery store. The strategy is smart when shopping elsewhere too. Every month there is a present you need to buy for a birthday, baby shower, or wedding, or there is an event that requires a new outfit. Whatever the reason that has you on the hunt for stuff, forgo top brands, unless you're getting them at a deep discount from the outlets or discount retailers. At the very least, you should be able to save around $250 a month.

Be Smarter About Using Credit Cards

When you use certain credit cards wisely (that means paying off your balance every month), you can save up real cash. Just like the grocery cards we mentioned above, issuers will reward you for your spending with cash back or rewards. If you don't get distracted and spend money just to get a deal, you can earn funds on money you would spend anyway. For instance, some popular cashback programs will give you as much as 5% back on up to $1,500 each quarter (on certain purchases that change every three months). So at a minimum, that's another $25 in your wallet each month.

Optimize Your Cell Phone Bill

Many of us pick a cell phone plan, then never check to see if it's the right one for us based on our usage, because the average cell phone bill is about $50, that's $600 per year of money you can optimize.

When buying a new cell phone, you likes to pay a little bit more upfront by choosing the unlimited data and text messaging plan. You then sets a three-month check-in on his calendar, and analyzes his spending patterns after a few months to see where you can cut back. You can use this method for any usage-based services.

Estimated savings: $20 to $600.

Create a 'No Spending' Day Once A Week

Choose one day each week and challenge yourself to not spend a single dollar.

Technically, even if you don't open your wallet, you're still spending money on things like rent, car insurance, and subscriptions, You just didn't count them. But that's even more of a reason to create a 'no spending' day on the money in your wallet: because you can actively control it.

The key to this tip is putting it in your calendar so it becomes a consistent system.

Estimated savings: $5 to $75.

Sell One Thing On eBay

If you're already doing a good job of saving, the next step is to make money.

This tip serves two main purposes. To symbolize to yourself that you can sacrifice by selling something, and to symbolize that you can make more money than your standard income. Once you do that, there are many other ways to generate income."

It doesn't matter what, or how many things, you sell. The point is not even to make much money (that's an added bonus). "The point is the symbolism of cleaning your life and generating even a small amount more money than you normally earn," he writes.

Estimated savings: $40 to $100.

Only Buy Something New When You're Replacing Something Old

By establishing a rule that you can only buy to replace something you already have, you're creating what it is call an "active barrier."

"Before buying anything, think 'how many of those do I need?' and, 'how many do I already have?' Then think again if you really need a new one," he advises. "The psychology of having to open up your closet, decide what to give away, and get it to the nearest charity (or garbage can) is enough to stop many of us from buying something new."

Estimated savings: From $10 to however much you would have bought otherwise.

Use Psychological Barriers To Prevent Yourself From Spending Money

If you find yourself eating out too much, stuff your fridge with perishables that you have to eat before they go bad. If you spend too much on shopping, unsubscribe from magazines or email lists that make it easier to make purchases.

The simple fact is, if things are automatic, you will do them. Don't just look for where you're spending today. That's surface-level. Look deeper to see what's causing you to spend, and if you decide you don't want to continue, then eliminate those causes.

Estimated savings: $10 to $200.

Pay Money To Save Money

It can seem counterintuitive to make purchases to save, but that's what some of the most successful money-savers do; they're not just buying things, they're investing in things tools and services that will eventually save them money over time.

It's transparently easy to see money going out of your pocket right NOW, but it's harder to understand that you're actually investing in yourself. And when you invest in yourself, there's no upper bound on what your return can be."

Estimated savings: $50 to $1,000.

Use The Free Rewards From Your Credit Card, Car Insurance, and Workplace

Think about the places you belong to as a member: your credit card, auto insurance, Costco, or your job. Each of these offers perks that most people ignore. By simply being a member, you get perks that can add up to thousands of dollars each year. To use this tip effectively, figure out exactly what your memberships offer. For example, some car insurance offers discounts on major retailers, and credit cards often offer travel insurance and car-rental discounts.

If anything stands out, set a calendar reminder for when it will apply. Another good rule of thumb is to always check for perks before you make any big purchases.
Estimated savings: $100 to $2,000.

Earn More Money Using a Skill You Already Have

Most Americans only think about cutting costs, resulting in frugality websites that frantically try to out-do each other with the most inane and meaningless tips of all. "We forget about the lever of earning more money, which is the most powerful of all. Try negotiating your salary at work, starting a second job, or freelancing for something you're very good at.
Estimated savings: $100 to $1,000.

Use Coupons

Vow to always use coupons, and not just on your groceries. With sites like Groupon and LivingSocial, you can snag deep discounts at local retailers. And if you're shopping online, always do a quick search for a coupon code before you check out. Sites like RetailMeNot and SlickDeals post coupon codes and special offers daily. You can also check out our deals page.

Coupons are Not as Untrendy as You Think

The thought of clipping coupons definitely sounds very untrendy, but let's face it in these times saving money is just cool and coupons are an excellent way to do it. For the larger national restaurants the weekly newspaper can be a good place to find coupons. You may also be surprised that local restaurants also offer coupons in local newspaper and local coupon booklets. It only takes a minute to save. Simply flip through the coupons and see if any catch your eye. Simply place the coupon in your wallet then next time you are around time and get the urge to stop by your favorite restaurant you will be ready to save. If you want to take your use of coupons to the next level you can use a envelope of small plastic folder to collect your coupons and keep it in your car so they are always nearby and ready for use.

Don't Ignore the Surveys

At several national chain and fast food restaurants there are now surveys on the receipts that offer chances to win money and prizes. The majority of people will simply ignore these offers, but this could be a great opportunity to get some cash back if. If you read these offers you will see that the potential to win can be substantial. I recently saw one that said that you could win up to $1,000 just by filling out a survey. Now since we know that only a fraction of people are going be filling out these surveys and it only takes a moment of time this is not a bad use of our time. One good way to do this is to save a couple of these receipts with surveys and fill them out at once. It shouldn't take more than 10 minutes and you could potentially win $1,000s of dollars. Be careful though as some of these surveys expire within just a few days. It is not likely that you will win anything right away, but if you make it a practice you can dramatically increase your chances of winning.

In today's busy world you may not be able to implement all of these tips but hopefully one or two of these ideas interested you as by doing just a few of them you could potentially save thousands of dollars per month.

How to save A thousand dollars per month on Groceries

The money you spend on food makes up a large portion of your weekly budget, so every dollar you can save at the supermarket really counts. Here are some tips to guide on saving $1,000 every month on how to spend less on groceries.

Save Money on Groceries at Home

Saving on groceries starts before you even leave the house.

Use what you have before buying more

You've already paid for everything in your cabinets, and if you're not using it, you're just throwing money away. Try to think of meals you can prepare using the ingredients you already have. Every extra meal you can squeeze out of these food items is one less you have to buy at the store.

Get the most out of the food you prepare

Leftovers can really save a family money in their food budget. It's like getting two meals for the price of one! If you cook a very large meal, consider freezing it in single portion containers. It will last longer and you'll probably appreciate the convenience factor of having a premade meal on hand when you don't have time to prepare a fresh one.

Plan a menu

When it comes time to go food shopping, prepare a menu for the week before you leave, using your store's flyer as a guide. This will help you take advantage of the week's best values and minimize unnecessary purchases once you get to the store. You'll probably also get your shopping done faster if you know exactly what you're looking for before you even get there.

Get the Best Price

Once you know what you need, it's important to get the best price possible.

Look for sales and coupons

You probably don't have time to look for every coupon available or travel from store to store to save a few cents on single food items, so don't go crazy here. Use coupons only for items you buy all the time, and don't fall for a deal just because it sounds good. Oftentimes, one brand with a coupon is still more expensive than another, less popular brand that doesn't come with a discount. You don't want to spend money just to get a price break on an item you don't need and are unlikely to use.

Get a store card
Most grocery stores have loyalty cards that you'll need to take advantage of the sales. Also, consider scanning your own groceries if your store has the option or sign up for your store's mobile app supermarkets are increasingly offering exclusive discounts to customers who use scanners and smartphones.

Use a credit card that offers cash back rewards on groceries
You can earn extra money for your hard work at the grocery store when you use a cash back credit card that offers a higher reward rate on grocery purchases. As long as you pay off your cards every month, you might as well as take advantage of getting something back for your weekly shopping trip.

Ways to Save Money While Shopping in Grocery Stores

Here are some tried and true tips and tricks that will save you money no matter where you shop.

Check unit prices

Many stores will list unit prices next to the price you'll pay to purchase the item, but don't be afraid to do the math if your store doesn't provide this convenience. Bring a calculator if you need to. The goal is to pay the lowest unit price possible, so compare between brands and container sizes.

Buy generic

Store brands are just as good as name brands for most items, and they're a lot cheaper. If the only reason you want the brand-name version is because of how it looks, try the generic alternative.

Look toward the top and bottom of shelves

Stores place the items they want you to purchase in the sections of the shelves that are easiest to reach. They want you to purchase these items because they have the highest markups, which means the store makes more money on them and you spend more money than you need to. Better buys are usually located on the higher and lower shelves in the aisle.

Minimize purchases of convenience foods

It's pretty common knowledge that buying premade frozen meals and other pre-prepared foods will cost you more than buying and preparing the ingredients yourself. Seemingly simple conveniences can cost you as well, though. Pre-sliced foods, or foods that are pre-separated into portions probably cost more than the small added convenience is worth.

Avoid single serving items

Individual packages of snacks and other foods will cost more than they do in their aggregate form. Small, single serving bags of chips will cost more than the same amount of chips in one large bag, for example. Purchase the larger version and separate the portions at home.

Buy in-season fruit and vegetables

It's very true that purchasing fresh, healthy foods at the grocery store is more expensive than purchasing processed foods with less nutritional value. Some of that cost can be offset by limiting your produce purchases to items that are in season. But when your favorite fruit and vegetables are not in season, consider buying frozen food. Picked when they're at their peak, frozen produce tastes almost as good as in-season food and is easy to prepare.

Purchases Patters To Avoid

Don't be enticed to spend more than you need to on your weekly shopping trip.

Avoid impulse buys

These are the purchases that eat your budget, so try not to make unplanned purchases when grocery shopping. Kids tend to increase impulse buying, so if at all possible leave them home. Small items like candy, gum, and magazines that line checkout aisles are attempts by your local store to squeeze a few more dollars out of you. Don't give in.

Eat before you shop

Shopping hungry will result not only in impulse buying, but probably also in over purchasing in the amount of food you'll need for the week. Never shop on an empty stomach.

Only buy groceries

Don't buy personal products like toothpaste or shampoo from a grocery store. You'll get better prices from larger stores like WalMart or Target, or even from your local dollar store. Cold cuts and other deli products are also better purchased at a deli than a grocery store. You'll get better prices and possibly better quality as well.

Don't buy small if you can buy in bulk

If you have a membership to a bulk store like Costco or Sam's Club, make sure to take advantage of the savings it offers. Don't purchase items in small quantities at the grocery store that you can purchase in bulk at lower unit costs using your membership card.

Follow the above tips, and you should be able to save a few dollars up thousands of dollar off your grocery bill each time you shop. It may not seem significant at the time, but every dollar counts. Most people grocery shop at least once a week, so you should notice a difference in your wallet after a few months.

Ways you use Waste dollar rather than saving it

You work hard for your money and you want to make sure you aren't wasting it. But over and over again, you are probably doing just that, in the form of unnecessary fees and purchases. I personally to took my time to studied myself and others to reveals the frequent money wasters and the ways to avoid them.

Extended Warranties

Consumer Reports surveyed thousands of car owners, and most of them found they paid a lot more for their extended warranties than they got back in savings when it came to repairs. Some people never needed the extended warranties at all. Others found that the repairs they needed weren't even covered.

The same issue comes up with extended warranties on other big-ticket items around your home. While a warranty that covers your electronics or appliances sounds helpful, it won't do you much good if you don't use the items very much or if the warranty costs more than the service charge to repair the item.

What you should do
You may automatically get an extended warranty when you purchase a big-ticket item, such as a computer or an appliance, with your credit card. Exclusions apply, of course, but many credit cards do offer this perk, which will cover the cost of an item that breaks down in the early stages. Save your receipts and warranty info, and check with your credit card company. Also think about the likelihood of the item falling apart before the agreement expires (for example, if you're single, your dishwasher may last you longer than, for example, a family of five that runs the dishwasher three times a day.)

Paying More Than You Have To On Gas
You might think it's better to put premium gasoline in your car because you think it contains more cleaning additive than regular unleaded gasoline. That sounds like a good theory, but it is not necessarily true. In fact, all octane grades include additives. Go by your owner's manual. If it suggests premium, use it. But if it doesn't, don't feel bad about keeping the extra money. Your car probably doesn't need it.

What you should do
Look into ways you can save a few bucks by signing up for rewards cards that shave off your price-per-gallon, or gas rewards credit cards that give you cash back for this purchase that you have to make anyway.

The Cost of Brand-Name Items

Generic brand cereal and milk are cheaper than name brands, usually by at least a dollar, but for some reason many of us can't ignore the familiar, fancier logo of a recognizable brand. We fall for it repeatedly even though oftentimes the difference between a generic and brand name product is just the packaging. The ingredients may be similar.

You'll gain the most cost savings going generic with prescription drugs. The FDA estimates that buying a generic brand prescription drug can save you 80% to 85% over the cost of a name brand prescription drug, on average. That is a substantial savings.

What you should do
Take time to compare products by going over the ingredient list. Don't tell your family members, and see if they notice the difference. And if they don't, you'll end up with more money in the family budget.

Uused Memberships

Gym memberships are great but only if you go to the gym regularly. Gym owners know this that's why they tend to put members on a payment plan that automatically pulls monthly fees from their credit card or bank accounts. These charges can be as high as $50 to $100 per month.

What you should do
Regularly review your credit card statements to check for any recurring charges you may have forgotten. And if you're not passionate about the gym, then make your own workout space at home or take up outdoor activities, like running, which don't cost more than the price of sneakers.

That New Car Smell

New cars have a certain allure; they're shiny, so clean, and you get to take in that brand-new car smell every time you get in the driver's seat. But those perks soon wear off while your hefty auto loan won't. The thing is, your new car will not stay new for long. In fact, as soon as you drive your car off the car lot, it's a used car.

Edmunds.com gives the lowdown with a quick example. A new Nissan 370z has a True Market Value (TVM) of $29,873. As you drive off the lot, your new car depreciates by more than $2,500.

What you should do
For the most part, you'll get a better deal by sticking to the used car lot. Do your research.

Credit-Monitoring Fees

Paying for credit monitoring through one of the three major credit bureaus can cost upward of $200 per year. You can check up on your credit for free, though, through AnnualCreditReport.com as federal law allows you to get a free copy of your credit report from each of the three credit reporting companies every 12 months.

That's not to say that credit monitoring isn't useful. It's good if you want daily access to your credit reports and instant notification if there are any changes, especially good if you've been a victim of identity theft. It isn't cheap, though. Expect to pay $169 for Experian (12 months), $215 for TransUnion (12 months) and $155 for Equifax (12 months). For the average consumer, the cost usually isn't worth it.

What you should do
If you're not worried about ID theft on a daily basis, save your money. Be careful when checking your credit score, though,

so that you don't inadvertently sign up for a credit-monitoring service.

Unnecessary Insurrance Coverage

When renting a car, the representative will ask you to accept or decline rental car insurance. The thought of damaging the vehicle and having to pay out of pocket races through your mind. But stop for just a second. Your current car insurance probably already covers you. Before you sign on the dotted line, check with your insurance carrier to make sure. Your credit card company may also cover you for rental cars.

What you should do
Before you hit the road, check with your Credit Card Company and current insurance carriers to find out if you are already covered.

Items You Won't Use

Did you buy that purple-collared shirt because you needed it or because it was on sale? Next time the clearance rack tempts you into buying something, question whether you're buying the item just for the thrill of getting a deal. The same goes for coupons. It's great to snag a high dollar coupon for something your family commonly consumes, but it's great only if you're actually going to use the product. If you are just buying something because of the price, you're simply throwing your money out the window.

What you should do
Take a moment to picture yourself using the product. If the image is fuzzy, put it back.

Impulse Buys

Whether you grab an extra bag of chips toward the end of your grocery store trip or pick up a soda on the way out of the gas station, it's impulse buying. Retailers know they can tempt you by putting items in a bin close to the checkout counter when you have less time to second-guess your purchases.

What you should do
Practice the walk-away test. Stick to your shopping list and walk away for at least 10 minutes when you suddenly feel compelled to buy something that's not on your list. You may forget all about it after the time has passed.

Interest Charges

You knew we'd get to this one eventually, right? Last but not least, we have to mention interest charges - those charges and penalties credit card companies and other creditors will apply whenever you keep a balance. While some interest rates are much lower than others (like student loans, which tend to have large balances that naturally take a long time to pay down), credit card interest rates tend to be hefty. If you pay only the minimum balance each month, those interest charges will quickly multiply, pushing you deeper into debt.

What you should do
Always pay attention to the box on your credit card statement that shows you how long it will take you to pay off your balance if you pay only the minimum balance. If you have already fallen into "the minimum payment trap," look into doing a balance transfer to another card to see if you can get a better rate (which would help you pay down your debt faster). And ideally, do away with those unnecessary and costly interest charges altogether. But if you must keep a balance, consider switching cards to one with a low interest rate.

Ways you Flushed Money Down the Toilet Today

We all make bad choices every day. Many of them take a direct hit on our finances. Stop flushing your money down the proverbial toilet, and put an end to these money wasting habits.

You Ate Out For The Third Time This Week

According to the USDA, over 30% of meals are eaten away from home. We're not saying to skip dining out altogether, but do make an effort to cut back your trips to the takeout counter and get more creative.

Not crazy about cooking? Look up recipes that can last more than one night. For example, roast a chicken one night and make fancy chicken sandwiches with arugula and honey mustard two nights later. Make burgers and baked fries on Tuesday and then use the hamburger meat to make tacos on Thursday. If you do order out, put half of it aside for later in the week.

You got the super-size latte with foam and a 50 cent shot of espresso.

If you spend around $5 on coffee or latte (and many spend more) just three days a week, it can add up to over $700 per year. If it's your daily habit, it could easily cost you more than $1,000 annually. We won't bore you by telling you to make your own coffee and drag a thermos to work. Instead, pitch in with your coworkers to buy a fancy coffee machine and take turns as the office barista.

You paid just the minimum due on your credit card bill, again.

It's so tempting, we get it. The credit card bill has a much smaller number next to your full balance, and you feel strapped for cash. Resist the urge to pay only the minimum balance each month, and take a harder look at how much you can really put toward your bills. Those interest charges are just going to continue to climb. And when you do pay off your bills, you'll be able to reap rewards.

You Drove At 80 mph To Get To Work

You know a lead foot leads to wasted gas, so why do you do it? Slow down and ride closer to the speed limit to minimize your commuting costs. Look at your other monthly expenditures tied to your way to work that could be lowered. Could you park farther away, at a cheaper lot? Is it more economical to ride the bus, even if you do it just twice a week? Could you possibly bike or walk?

If you still can't resist the driving so quickly, then at least look into seeing whether the rewards from a gas credit card could offset your heavy right foot.

You Drank Half A Bottle Of Wine And It's Only Wednesday

If you smoke or drink, not only will your health take a hit, but your wallet will too. The USDA says that that people in the U.S. spend about 2% of their total expenditures on tobacco and alcohol, which adds up to over $700 on average. If tee totaling just isn't your thing, then think about cutting back to only the weekends.

You Chose Plastic Bottled Water

You don't need to be a math whiz to realize that spending $1 to $2 on each bottle of water is quite pricey. There are many home filters on the market, with technology ranging from carbon filtration to steam distillation. Find independent comparison data on different brands. Then, carry your water to the office in an eye-catching BPA-free bottle.

You Were Too Lazy To Cut Out A Coupon

There are two ways to use coupons— either for stuff you need and buy regularly or as an opportunity to try something new that you probably won't use. The latter leads to impulse buys. But the former is worth taking the time to do. Sign up for updates, by email or through social media, only for your most favorite brands. And take a moment to grab the flier at the front of the grocery store before you start shopping. Coupons may feel quaint, but if you're savvy about which ones you use, you could realize hefty savings.

You Let Your Belly Rumblings Prod You To The Vending Machine

Snacks from vending machines can cost 75 cents to $1.50 or more per snack or beverage. Daily, this can be as expensive as your bottled water habit. Or, if you're more likely to visit the little café or bakery near the office or campus, reward yourself with weekly instead of daily visits. For vending junk food junkies, here are some ideas to add to your workplace stash that are cheaper when bought ahead of time at the supermarket:

- Small bags of chips or crackers

- Juice or flavored milk or coffee 6-packs
- Box of granola or snack bars
- 4 or 6-pack yogurts
- Dried fruit snacks
- Veggie or fruit and dip packs

You Spent Half An Hour Reading About Things You Already Know

Buying magazines on impulse at the checkout corner is a waste. You were probably won over by a sensational headline about a topic you've already read about 20 times. Stick to only your favorite publications and subscribe to them during a fundraising event or through your tablet for cheaper subscriptions. Another option is to go to your local library as they likely have most of your magazines there that you can browse anytime.

You lied when your spouse asked about the last time you got an oil change.

How conscientious are you about little decisions you make each day? Do you reach for healthy snacks instead of potato chips? Does your car and home receive scheduled maintenance? Taking care of yourself and your valuable assets could save you money on everything from healthcare to major repairs.

Reasons you need to save up Money for Future

At the end of every month, it's always the same question, how much did you manage to save? But then, the thought also crosses your mind... Why the need to save, when you earn to spend? If you find yourself cash strapped, there's the always the option of borrowing some money.

Different people save for different reasons. We've discussed 5 reasons you need to start setting aside a few dollars each month.

Emergency Funding

Emergencies are unexpected and uncalled for. A family member might take ill, your roof might start leaking or your drain pipes might get clogged, your car might be involved in an accident or you might have to make an emergency trip. It's worse if you get laid.

It is impossible to tide over these unexpected expenses if you don't have any savings to fall back on. So, that's one reason you need to start saving money.

Retire In Peace

This is why most people save money. After working everyday of your life, you dream of living those days of retirement in peace and comfort. You don't want to be paying up debts until the end. Neither do you want to take up a part time job to make ends meet for your family.

You can always consult a financial advisor or coach and chalk out a savings plan for your retirement. You can invest your money in places with high returns.

Fewer Debts

Credit is easy to obtain today, but it's not without the condition of repayment. If you keep borrowing for every unexpected expense, you take on more and more debt making it hard to meet those monthly payments. With reserve fund, you can pay up a few expenses against your credit card and the rest from your savings. At the end of it, you will have a great credit score.

Building a reserve fund will also keep tabs on your spending habits.

Financial Independence

When you have your own spending money, you can call your own shots. You can make choices for your own life. You can decide to quit your dead end job and enroll at college for a course you've always wanted to take. You can buy new furniture for your home or take an exotic vacation with your family.

Buying a House

Buying a house is a dream come true for many. You can get a loan to pay up for your house, but you are still required to contribute at least 10%-20% towards the cost. In other words, you have to pay the down payment if you want your loan sanctioned. Your savings can come handy for this initial payment and also to cover up any additional costs and fees.

The scenario is the same if you are planning to gift yourself a new car.

Given these five reasons, you might also have to save for your kid's education; higher education is not cheap. By pinching a few pennies early, you will be able to guarantee your kids a good college education.

Saving money every month is easier said than done. Some unexpected expense crops up and the money just slips away. If you find it hard to save money and keep track of your monthly budget, here's help in the form of a financial coach.

Ways To $1,000 per month Save Money in college

Ever hear the phrase "starving student?" Well, it didn't come from nowhere (and certainly not a fat-cat). College students are notoriously broke, but it doesn't have to be that way. These tips will put up to $1,000 per month or more in your pocket. Regardless of whether you are a student or not, these tips will help you save money or think like a student who can save money.

Make a Budget, Check It Twice

This is number one on our list for a reason. It's easy to let money fritter away. Thou Shalt Not Fritter. A nightclub cover charge here, a dinner out with friends there, a book you didn't know you had to buy for class thrown in the mix and suddenly all the money you have for the month vanishes in a cloud of shame. Getting a basic idea of how much you're spending each month and where you can cut back is one of the most fundamental financial lessons you'll learn while in college. This worksheet will help you brainstorm your expenses while Mint.com can track your spending.

Rule the School

Aside from tuition, room and board are going to be your next biggest expense. At some schools, room and board costs even more than tuition. Hey, they've got to pay for those ungodly expensive dorms somehow. Students who work as Resident Advisors frequently get free or significantly reduced room and board in exchange for their work. Considering that the average full-time student attending an in-state public school pays $8,535 per year in room and board according to The College Board, working as an RA can be one of the most lucrative gigs on campus to save up $1,000 per month.

Recycle

It happens every year unwitting freshmen buy hundreds of dollars worth of text books then virtually cry at the end of the semester when they're worthless. Watch the faces of students in line at the book store. The ones who look devastated are those who haven't figured out that textbooks are expensive as heck and get sold back for pennies on the dollar.

The College Board reports that the average student pays $1,137 for books and supplies every year, but you can check the same books out of your library for free. If the campus library isn't an option, sites like eCampus, Chegg, and CollegeBook Renter will rent you books for a semester while sharing with a friend can cut the cost of buying books in half.

Shack Up
Three's a crowd right? Come and knock on our door. It's also a cheaper living situation. Students who live with more roommates in dorms equipped with fewer amenities typically pay less than those who live alone in posh campus pads. It's not uncommon for the cheapest dorms on a campus to cost 20-30 percent less than the priciest.

Cook It Up
College is all about learning about self-discovery, whether it's in a mind-blowing anthropology class, being away from your parents for the first time or realizing that hey, you actually don't eat the same thing as the linebacker who lives down the hall. (And scholarship money pays for his eats anyway.)

Schools accommodate by offering several meal plan options, which can vary by up to $1,000 per year in price. While many schools require those living on-campus to purchase a meal plan, students can typically choose whether they want a large or small option. Prepping some of your meals at home can save a bundle both during and after college. And by the way, been to WalMart lately?

Shop Around

Yes, it's undeniably cooler to be living with your friends in a pad far removed from resident advisors' watchful eyes, but living off-campus can cost anywhere from 10 to 40 percent more than the dorm life. In addition to forking over cash for utilities, students who live off-campus also pay for phone, internet connections, commuter parking passes, furniture, a security deposit and summer months when they may or may not live in their apartments. Think carefully before signing a lease.

Free Yourself

Those tens of thousands of dollars that you fork over every year they pay for much more than just your classes. Campuses are chock full of "free" amenities that come with your tuition including on-campus entertainment, movie rentals from the library, gym membership, intramural sports activities, dorm dinners, guest lecture series and student clubs. Take advantage of these. The College Board reports that the average on-campus student spends

$1,989 per year on "personal expenses," much of which is entertainment they could have gotten for free from their school.

Rent, Rent, Rent
That loft and mini-fridge you're eyeing for your dorm? You're probably not going to use them after college. Some schools have low-cost rental program for amenities like vacuums and hot pots. If that's not an option at your school, don't sweat it. Companies like Loft Concepts and Bedloft will rent and deliver.

Reciprocate
First reciprocate. Then do it again. Academic reciprocation agreements are the ugly step-sibling of scholarships and grants. Under-publicized and virtually unknown, agreements like the Western Undergraduate Exchange, the Midwest Higher Education Compact and the Academic Common Market maintain relationships with bordering nearby states that basically allow out-of-state students in partner states to attend college without paying the full out-of-state fees. That means that if you attend a Virginia public college and want to major in something that isn't offered in the state, you can fly your pasty butt

down to Florida if there's a public college that offers your major there.

While the Midwest Higher Education Compact and the Academic Common Market are only open to students in specific programs of study namely programs that aren't available in the student's home state the Western Undergraduate Exchange is open to students in "virtually all undergraduate fields." If you live in a border county and attend college just over the state line, your school may offer an out-of-state reduction for those living in your county. The College Board reports that the average out-of-state fee for a full-time student is $11,990 per year. A little research and a call to your financial aid office can save you more than $47,600 over the course of your college tenure.

Plan Ahead

You know all of those college movies where students get into college, do their thing and graduate in four short years before they know it? That's not how it goes down in the real world. Statistically, only about one-third of full-time students seeking a bachelor's degree graduate in four years reports the National Center for Education Statistics. Even more scary, just over half graduate in six years. That's two years past the point when your parents said they would cut off funding. Talking to your advisor and planning your college tenure can literally cut tens of thousands off of your college bill.

Maximize Summer

Summer school is a drag but so is ponying up for yet another semester. Streamline your college tenure correctly and you could get out in three rather than four years. Or at least have time to chill. Summer school, community college classes, internships, AP and CLEP exams and summer study abroad programs can all save money by helping you graduate faster. A course at a major university costs (using some cost accounting guessing here) 3 grand. That same course can be box-checked at the local Harvard-on-the-hill JC for 300 bucks. Or less.

Start Small

Nobody makes movies that glorify the two-year college experience. And we don't mean the fine work by Kim Kardashian. That's because the community college experience is not even close to the four-year college experience. Community and two-year colleges cost a mere pittance of their four-year rivals $2,713 on average versus $16,140 at a public college or

$36,993 at a private one but don't have the same lavish campuses, research facilities or highly published profs. If you can deal with the bare bones amenities for a couple of years, you can transfer to the four-year school of your dreams with more money in your pocket.

Stay Put

Once you've made it to a four-year institution, stay there until you graduate. Students who transfer from one four-year school to another lose an average of one full semester's worth of credits. Unless you're transferring from a super pricey school to a substantially cheaper one, it usually makes more financial sense to stay where you are.

Carpool

Math time: 1 trip to and from campus every day x 20 school days per month + 150 miles home once a month + a 200 mile weekend road trip with your friends + 6 grocery runs because hey, your friends don't have cars + that trip to the mall + two trips to get your roomie's car back from campus towing .... a lot of driving.

Like spending, driving sneaks up on you. Before you know it, you've spent more on gas than you did on books this semester. Why should you have to pay for gas on those car trips? Many colleges offer ride boards that hook bill-paying passengers up with drivers headed to the same destination. If your school doesn't have its own ride board, this site can hook you up.

Give Back
Baby, give back. While your friends are making bad decisions in Cancun, you're feeding the hungry, tutoring at-risk kids or helping Mother Earth. Alternative Spring Break programs connect college groups with needy organizations and offer a vastly cheaper way to spend your spring break. The experience is...different. Instead of partying their eyeballs out, ASBers do volunteer work during the day, spend their nights exploring their destinations and crash on the floors of other volunteers' homes and generous nonprofits. If your school doesn't offer an ASB chapter, start one or check out trips through neighboring colleges and universities.

Trade In
Exchanging a private for a federal student loan is like trading a unicycle for a jet. Cheaper and armed with far better borrower benefits, federal student loans are almost laughably superior to their private loan counterparts (here's a full

explanation why). While federal student loans are capped at a modest 6.8% (subsidized Stafford Loans are capped for 2011-2012 at a ridiculously low 3.4%), private student loans can easily reach 15% or even 18% plus origination and administration fees. A student who takes out a $20,000 Stafford Loan at a 6.8% interest will pay $11,101 less over the life of the loan than a student who takes out a pricey private loan.

If you have private loans but haven't maxed out your federal student loan options, switching to federal loans next year will be one of the best financial decisions you've ever made. The federal Stafford Loan program allows all dependent students to borrow up to $27,000 over four years while the Perkins Loan will provide an extra $27,000 for needy students.

Pay the Interest

Paying interest pays off. That's because every year you're in school, your student loan interest slowly gets bigger. Wait long enough and you'll have to pay interest on the interest. The good news is that you can sidestep all of that fiscal inkiness by simply paying a little bit towards you interest each month. If two freshmen each take out $5,500 Stafford Loans the maximum you can borrow during your first year of college but

Student A pays the paltry $31 in interest the loan accrues each month, they'll leave school with a loan that's $1,500 lower than a student who let the interest accumulate.

Can It on Credit

How many times have we told you that spending can sneak up on you faster than a ninja on steroids? At least three in this article alone. Thanks in large part to not having any idea how much they're charging, the average college student graduates with $2,200 in credit card debt on top of student loans.

Credit cards, especially high-interest ones issued to starving college kids, can spiral out of control pretty easily. Think of it this way if you charge a $15 pizza on a card with an 18% interest rate during your freshman year, you'll pay more than double for that pizza by the time you're a senior. Reserve those cards for emergencies only and pay them off ASAP.

Work Hard

Good grades and close ties to your department advisors will not only make job hunting and recommendation-getting a cakewalk when you're a senior, it will also help you land scholarships and grants reserved for upperclassmen. Most colleges have special aid awards designed to reward students who have busted their rump academically, athletically or extra curricularly (that's totally a real word) as well as paid research and assistantship positions for juniors and seniors. Do well, keep in touch with the financial aid office, check with your department heads and coaches about aid for upperclassmen and peruse Shmoop's Scholarship Database. It will literally pay off.

Tap Hidden Money Resources
Grants and scholarships aren't the only ways to pay for college. "Alternative aid" options ranging from tuition waiver programs to national service awards can foot your bill just as easily. What's this "alternative aid" we speak of? Check out Shmoop's list.

Ask for More
Death, divorce, medical expenses...things happen and financial aid offices understand that. If your family's financial circumstance changes while you're in college, you may be eligible for more financial aid. Situations like job loss or other surprise bills won't show up on your financial aid forms. If you encounter an unexpected change, head straight to your school's financial

aid office and request a professional judgment. It's not guaranteed that your school will hand over a bigger chunk of change, but it's worth a shot.

Access Student Discounts

Smile, get your student ID then use it until you can no longer pass for 21. Your student ID grants you discounts on items ranging from movie tickets to computers. Student discounts are particularly advantageous when it comes to traveling. Amtrak and Greyhound both offer discounts for student travelers while STA Travel can hook you up cheapo with flights.

Get Personal With the Career Center

You've slogged through four years (or more) of exams, research projects and theses. You've finally turned the tassel. You've graduated! And made it to the real world!...only to be jobless and bored out of your mind for the next half a year. That exact scenario happens all the time. The University of California Santa Barbara Career Center reports that the average job search for new college grads takes 3 to 6 months, meaning that it could be quite a while after you leave college before you can start paying your student loans back.

A quick visit to your campus career center can help you research jobs other grads in your field have landed, connect with recruiters and land a full-time gig before you graduate. Career centers frequently sponsor job fairs, resume critique workshops, mock interview sessions, networking resources, connections to professional organizations in your field and job shadowing opportunities. Take advantage of them while they're free.

Work it Off

If that last scenario sends chills up your spine, it should. Post-grad joblessness is no joke, especially when you've got student loans. Luckily there are steps you can take to reduce your risk of winding up over educated and under employed.

Research from the National Association of Colleges and Employers shows that 2 out of every 5 interns are offered a full-time job once their internship is over. Internships get a bad rap because many of them are unpaid, but there are some very lucrative gigs. Find one, do well and walk away with a post-grad job along with jealous looks from your broke friends.

Ways College Students can save $1,000 per month before Class Starts

College tuition and housing is expensive enough on its own. But then you start adding up all of the other college costs, both in and out of the classroom, and things can become quite overwhelming. Fortunately, there are ways to save significant money on expenses if you do some planning and look for out-of-the-box ways to save.

Buy Textbooks Used

News alert: Brand new college textbooks are really, really expensive. Fortunately, the ease of shopping online has created an excellent way to buy gently used textbooks at a steep discount. We're talking over 75% off the retail price of new books and savings in the range of $1,000 over the course of an academic year. A few excellent online resources worth exploring include Chegg, eCampus.com, AbeBooks.com, BigWords.com, and even Barnes & Noble has entered the used textbook field.

You can also sell back used textbooks for a pretty decent return, so be sure to take care of the books as condition is a huge factor when determining how much you'll get back at the end of the semester. If you don't want to buy your books, you can also look into renting them for the semester and saving a good chunk of change in the process. A few resources worth exploring include TextbookRentals, BookRenter, and Amazon.

Ask About Student Discounts

When buying items like clothing, shoes, backpacks, and laptops in preparation for the upcoming school year, it would really benefit you to ask about student discounts. A few examples of discounts available include 20% off your order at Banana Republic, 15% off at J. Crew, and even 10% off at your local Goodwill. When it comes to buying tech, Best Buy, Apple Store, and Dell all have student-specific online programs that offer significant discounts. Apple, for example, is currently offering $200 off a new MacBook and up to $20 off an iPad.

Typically, all you need to get the discount is your student ID. If you're a freshman and don't have an ID yet, just bring along your registration letter, or something similar, to prove your student status. Make it a healthy habit to always ask about student discounts when shopping anywhere. Also, be sure to ask when dining out as many restaurants offer unadvertised discounts to students.

Find Free or Cheap Transportation

Many colleges and universities team up with local bus authorities to offer free bus rides for students. Many incoming students are not made aware of this. Speaking from my own experience, I was a sophomore in college before I realized I could ride the local bus for free. Once you get on campus, ask around about this possibly free, or highly discounted, transportation method. Not only will you save on gas, but you'll avoid all of the other costs that come with maintaining a vehicle while in school.

Call Your Roommate to Avoid Duplicate Purchases

I'll never forget showing up on campus and meeting my first college roommate. It turned out we had quite a bit in common, including ownership of a microwave, mini-fridge, and 27" tube TV. If only I had called him ahead of time to see what stuff he was bringing, it would have saved me significant money. After all, no dorm room ever built has enough room for all your stuff and it's silly not to share. Lesson learned the hard way.

Always communicate with your future roommate and determine what items you actually need to buy.

Choose the Meal Plan That Works for You

I can remember a friend during my college days who paid for three meals a day (21 meals a week) in the school cafeteria but typically only went 10-15 times per week. At the time, I figured we was blowing close to $50 a week on uneaten meals, not including the money he spent eating out and at the grocery store. Always consider your eating habits when deciding on the right meal plan for you. For example, if you tend to skip breakfast and grab a bagel on the way out the door, you'll want to adjust your meal plan accordingly. Also, if you like throwing a sandwich together for a light lunch and have classes scheduled during lunch hours, you'll want to adjust your plan as well. Bottom line, don't blindly sign up for a meal plan without considering how much of the plan you'll actually use.

Research the Best Cell Phone Plan

You can also save significant money by researching the best cell phone plan that meets your specific needs. Simply adding another line to a family plan is not always going to give you the best deal. Or perhaps you're in a situation where that is not even an option. If you tend to use very few talk minutes (100 or less per month), you should consider a T-Mobile prepaid plan. For a very affordable $30 a month, you get unlimited web and text, 5GB data at 4G speeds, and 100 talk minutes. I have this no-contract plan and absolutely love it.

If you're a big talker and texter, but don't necessarily need high-speed data because of free college Wi-Fi, consider Cricket Wireless. For only $25 per month, you get unlimited talk and text, all with no annual contract. If you need a data plan, you can upgrade to 2.5 GB for an additional $15 per month. You can either buy a phone directly from Cricket, or save money by scoring a deal on an unlocked used smartphone on eBay.

Set up the Right Student Checking Account

Never blindly accept the bank or checking account recommended by your school. In many cases, they're loaded with hidden fees and often times the college or university receives a kickback for promoting the bank, making it a biased recommendation. It's important to do some independent research and find the right checking account for you. Look for student checking accounts that have no fees for debit transactions, branches near campus so you avoid out-of-network ATM charges, and no monthly fees when a reasonable account balance is maintained.

Also, if you're comfortable doing your banking via your smartphone, consider using an online mobile bank like Capital One 360. The lack of physical branches is more than made up for by the lack of fees along with a decent interest rate. No overdraft fees, no minimum monthly balance required, and all completely FDIC insured. Are you worried about not being able to get quick access to cash? Don't be, as Capital One has over 2000 ATMs in addition to 38,000 fee-free ATMs account users can use. By doing your due diligence and researching frugal ways to save on college costs, you can definitely lower your stress level when it comes time to pay your monthly bills. After all, balancing college life and your studies can be stressful enough without worrying about finances too.

Resource

Create a Spending Plan

Draw a Spending Map So You Don't Get Lost

Putting your financial goals in writing can make them seem more concrete and achievable. However, it's easy to allow everyday purchases and obligations to get in the way of saving for the future. One of the best ways to make sure your daily spending habits don't overwhelm your life goals is to create a spending plan. A spending plan is not meant to be a strict budget. Instead, it's a guide that will help you take control of your financial future and, ultimately, reach your goals. To create your spending plan, follow these four steps:

Step One: Identify Income.

Step Two: List Expenses. (Review the Tracking Your Expenses Worksheet from Know Where Your Money Goes, or create one now if you don't have one.)

Step Three: Compare Income and Expenses.

Step Four: Set Priorities and Make Changes.

A Diet for Your Wallet!

Do you have a written household budget? If not...it's time to get you budget out of your head & onto paper! It's a simple fill in the blank exercise! You must know your budget before you can start a diet for your wallet!

Part 1

Do you have a written household budget?

If not...here's your weekly challenge: get your budget out of your head & onto paper!

Here's how...just start filling in the blanks! (keep in mind that some income & expenses may not apply to you...e.g. alimony!)

Step 1: Start with total monthly income:
- Salary
- Spouses salary
- Child support
- Alimony
- Other

Step 2: Next, list your monthly expenses:
- Mortgage/rent
- Insurance (auto, home, life, health, disability, dental, long term care)
- Car payments
- Child care
- Clothes

- Memberships (country club, pool or fitness center)
- Lessons (piano, dance, etc.)
- Cleaning service
- Lawn service
- Pool service
- Loans (home equity, student, credit cards)
- Savings (college, retirement, vacation, emergency)

***Some expenses (like the ones below) tend to fluctuate, so calculate the average monthly expenditure:
- Water / sewer
- Electricity
- Gas (not for your car, but your home)
- Internet
- Cell Phone
- Phone
- Cable or Satellite

Now the fun part...simply subtract your total monthly expenses from your total monthly income.

Take a long, hard look at this number because that's the amount you should be living on every month...food, fun, gas, dry cleaner & all those everyday expenses! Please keep in mind that the average family of four spends $800 - $1,000 per month just on food!

Let's suppose you have $2000 left to spend. Set aside 30% ($600 per month) for expenses that I refer to as "Oh No" expenses...car repairs, plumber, doctor visit, big gifts, etc. These expenses should not come from your "emergency" savings because these are not emergencies...they are just part of life, & they will come up every month! If you don't budget for them, you'll end up going into debt to take care of these expenses.

After you set aside $600 for "oh no" expenses, you'll have $1400 left or $350 per week...known as "weekly allowance"! Put your $350 weekly allowance in your wallet...spend wisely because when it's gone, it's gone!

Let's get this diet for your wallet started right now!

Part 2
Sometime your overspending requires your wallet to go on a **CRASH DIET!**
If you're in need of some serious savings, consider this your weekly challenge!

It's a simple 3-step process, here's how:
#1. You must know the amount of your weekly allowance

#2. Once you're used to spending your weekly allowance and not a penny more...let the crash diet begin!

#3. Starting this week, allow yourself to only spend half of your weekly allowance! Example: If your weekly allowance is $350, you're going to have to live on $175...food, fun, gas, dry cleaner, etc. Continue the crash diet for 4 weeks!

This is a tough challenge, but it will force you to change some spending habits & save a lot of money!

You'll have to think twice about every purchase and always shop for a bargain!

If grocery shopping is where you spend way too much... switch to buying only store brands and you'll save 25%!

If you're not a cook... consider these "no recipe required" dinner ideas: breakfast for dinner, taco bar, make your own burrito, pasta bar, baked potato bar (perfect for leftover BBQ or chili)!

If your idea of family fun requires you to spend a lot of money... you need to re-think your definition of fun! Think about parks, picnics, board games, puzzles & more!

Have a reward to make this challenge more fun. Take the money you save and buy something you really want or go on a weekend vacation. Get the entire family involved in this diet for your wallet!

Conclusion

Everyone is looking for ways to save money. There are many ways that you can save money, some are creative, some are subtle and some are... well extreme.

These are necessarily things that everyone would do or want to do. However, they are good tips because you never really know how tight you will have to keep your budget if you main source of income goes away tomorrow.

Yes, the thought may give you a headache but they can save you money, a lot of money. If you are facing tough economic times or you are just trying to prevent having a tough time consider my tips. Based on my figures if you strictly follows all guidelines you will save thousands of dollars per month.

This will force you to eat at home more and actually use the food in your cupboards and freezer. It will also make you keenly aware of what your spending habits are per month. You could easily save $1,000 a month or more.

Saving money doesn't have to be a chore. As you start discovering more and more ways to save, you will find that it comes easier as the months pass by. Plus, at the end of the year you'll have a big fat lump sum to look forward to.

Again, there are many ways to make an extra $1,000 a month. Some are a lot easier than others. But if you devote the time and effort to building it, there is no reason why you should not be saving whatever your goal is.

If you want to save more money, you have to start using your common sense. If you are trying to keep up with the Jones's, stop; because you will go broke. Always try to live within your means, or better yet, try living slightly below your means.

Assess how you are spending your money and whether it is totally necessary to buy the things you are buying. It boils down to your needs versus your wants. Just make sure that the things you buy are truly important, and don't spend more than you make.

Today I can save more than $1,000 per month. My strategy is to keep my expenses at the same level while my extra income will either go into my saving account or into my investment account. I invest in things that are valuable or in things that can grow overtime.

One Last Thing...

If you enjoyed this book or found it useful, I would be very grateful if you would post a short review on Amazon. Your support really does make a difference and I read all the review personally.

Thank You for Writing a Review on Amazon

Thank you again for your support and Happy Saving!

www.ingramcontent.com/pod-product-compliance
Lightning Source LLC
Chambersburg PA
CBHW060405190526
45169CB00002B/759